3D-PRINTING AND DIGITAL INFRINGEMENT: CHALLENGES TO EXISTING PATENT LAW

VOLUME 1, ISSUE 4 OF BRILLOPEDIA

VAISHALI SINGH

ISBN 979-888546638-7

Contents

Preface

"Start writing, no matter what. The water does not flow until the faucet is turned on".

-Louis L'Amour

Hundreds of students and professors are contributing their work to Brillopedia, we are here to provide ample information about Law and Contemporary issues. Our aim is to provide a platform for today's generation to express their views and ideas on law and contemporary law.

Author

Vaishali Singh

Publication

This research paper is published in volume 1, issue 4 of Brillopedia

ABSTRACT

The digital revolution has now moved beyond music and video files. A person can now translate three-dimensional objects into digital files and, at the press of a button, recreate those items via a 3D printer or similar device.3D printing isn't a "new" technology by any means, but it's fast becoming more affordable and accessible. For one, some of the historic licensing hurdles have been cleared from the field. Many of the key patents protecting pre-existing industrial printing processes are expiring. But the proliferation of 3D printing has also led to a number of novel intellectual property (IP) issues. Notably, 3D printing has made it easy to duplicate patented objects — and difficult to take legal action against infringers. As 3D printing enters the mainstream, it's important for patent holders to understand and prepare for the challenges that 3D printing presents to the existing patent system.

CHAPTER TWO

INTRODUCTION

The history of global manufacturing tells us how industrial revolution introduced the phenomenon of mass production of goods at lower costs, called the economies of scale. 3D- Printing, is the kind of technology that has the power to revolutionize the way things are manufactured completely.3-D Printing is no longer science fiction and it is being used to manufacture a variety of things such as hearing aids, jewellery, and even parts for NASA.[1]

The speed and precision of this technology is bound to be of great utility to many industries, such as, automotive, aerospace, agricultural machinery, consumer goods and so on.[2]Not just things, but now 3-D Printing is also being used for printing artificial body organs. A small start-up called Prellis Biologics, consists of a few scientists and interns who are conducting extensive research towards developing artificial yet functional body organs for humans. Looking at their progress it has been estimated that the global tissue engineering market will reach $94 billion by 2024, up from $23 billion in 2015.[3] Therefore it can be safely presumed that technological marvel of 3-D Printing is going to elevate the global organs and implants market to a new level. This technology is now available to anyone, which means anyone could turn their basement into a factory and build almost anything!

Since any one could now make anything, the implications of this technology on Intellectual Property Law are going to be drastic. Would using the 3-D printer, for printing out kitchenware, daily use objects, etc. infringe IP rights? Imagine the abundance of pirated products that can be produced through this technology. The first part of this paper includes a flashback to the evolution of 3D printing and the underlying technology as well as its presence in the industry today, that is, in India and other parts of the world. Subsequently, the second part of the paper will give a brief note on the implications of 3D printing technology on intellectual property law. The third part of the paper willanalyse the challenges that the traditional patent regime would face due to advancement of 3D printing technology, by establishing the current position in USA and need for changes in Indian Patent laws. The conclusion and suggestions will be focussed on development of an IP framework that would promote the growth of 3D Printing industry and also benefit the various stakeholders.

[1]Jennifer Stanfield, *NASA Tests First 3-D Printed Rocket Engine Part Made with Two Different Alloys*, NASA, Sept. 18, 2017, available at: https://www.nasa.gov/centers/marshall/news/news/releases/2017/nasa-tests-first-3-d-printed-rocket-engine-part-made-with-two-different-alloys.html.

[2] Peter Twomey, *A New Dimension to Intellectual Property Infringement: An Evaluation of the Intellectual Property Issues Associated with 3D Printing*, 17 Trinity C.L. Rev. 14 (2014).

[3]Jonathan Shieber, *Implantable 3D-printed organs could be coming sooner than you think*, TECHCRUNCH, June 26, 2018, available at: https://techcrunch.com/2018/06/25/implantable-3d-printed-organs-could-be-coming-sooner-than-you-think/.

EVOLUTION OF 3D PRINTING

The 3D Printing technology emerged nearly three decades ago, when an engineer named Charles Hull printed a small cup through a process called stereo lithography, wherein a liquid photo polymer substance is cured and glued together layer by layer using Ultra Violet Lighting till it hardens and takes shape of the object desired. He started a company called "3D Systems" in 1986, selling 3D printers, and the technology attracted some high-end companies like Mercedes Benz and General Motors.[1] Charles Hull was granted patent for his stereolithography apparatus in 1980. An Israel based company called Stratasys, brought in some competition in the industry in 1989. The process used by Stratasys was fuse deposition which was patented in1992, wherein melted modelling plastic is injected through nozzles layer by layer. The Selective Laser Sintering (SLS) process that is popular and widely used today, was patented by Carl Decker in 1989, who started his own 3D Printing start-up called Desk Top Manufacturing Corporationwith his professor at University of Texas. SLS is a process wherein the modelling material, whether plastic, glass etc. is heated using laser beams to form a hard 3D object. Desk Top Manufacturing was taken over by 3D Systems in 2001. The end of 1980s also saw the growth of a 3D Printing company in Europe called EOS systems which have also largely used the SLS technology to produce quality 3D objects. In 1990s, there were several other types of 3D Printing technologies that had come to market, but as of now only three company's technology, that is, 3D Systems, EOS and Stratasys have managed to survive till date. [2]

During 2000s, there wasn't any exponential growth in the 3D Printing industry, mainly because the technology was protected through Non-Disclosure Agreements, leading to mostly high-end 3D technology being used in Automotive, Aerospace, Jewellery and Medical industries. The technology couldn't reach the lower end markets because of it being less user-friendly and cost effective. Therefore, the market did not see much of a fundamental change till 2009, when the first 3D Printer for commercial use called the Cupcake CNC, arrived[3]. It was the first affordable home 3D Printer, created by MakerBot, a start-up that believed in the open source 3D Printing movement. Their printer used a process that was somewhat similar to Fuse Disposition technique, but could print with much more speed and was cost effective. MakerBot was taken over by Stratasys in 2013.[4]

In the current scenario the major global players in 3D Printing industry apart from Stratasys, EOS and 3D Systems are, Arcam, a Swedish company that has grown a substantially large global market for itself in orthopaedic implants and aerospace industry. Renishaw, which has focussed most of the application of its Additive Manufacturing technology to dental industry. Optomec, Organovo which is a bioprinter and Voxeljet are newer smaller companies that are slowly gaining momentum in the 3D Printing industry. [5] The growth in the industry is quite noticeable, because of the large number of newcomers entering the market. According to a expert analyst in the field of 3D Printing, the growth in this industry has seen a decent raise from 17% in 2016 to 25% this year, that is, on just two year.[6]Another important factor that has encouraged more start-ups in 3D Printing technology is the fact that many patents that were registered some 20-30 years ago, that cover the basic technology underlying 3D Printing have already expired by 2014 or 2015. Thus, a lot of information has been available for open access since past 3 years.[7]

Coming to the scenario in India, the country has seen tremendous rise in the number of start-ups and innovation, in last one decade. However, there only few start-ups in the country that deal with 3D Printing products. There are numerous challenges that Indian 3D Printing industry faces. Most notable issue is that there is not much awareness or research in the field of 3D Printing technology. And, the business also involves huge capital investment as a result of which the products are also overpriced which does not attract a major chunk of Indian market.[8]

• **THE UNDERLYING TECHNOLOGY**

The 3D Printing technology, simply stated, is nothing but a machine that can convert blueprints of a design into 3D objects.[9] Therefore, the first step of the process is creating the blueprint of the object one wants to create. A blueprint can be created through any modelling software, that is a Computer Aided Design (CAD) program available online. There is also a website that showcases various products that have been designed for 3D Printing by other people. One can simply download the designs of a product they like from Thingverse[10] for free, and make as many copies of it as they like. The CAD file is the sent to the printer which will either through laser sintering or fuse depositing processes (depending on the kind of 3D printer one buys), convert the virtual design into a real time physical object. A 3D Printer can be used to create a vast number of daily use objects, such as, mugs, cups, jars, toys, fashionable jewellery, shoes etc. Plastic is the most common material used by the 3D Printers, though, there are printers that can make metal and ceramic objects using the laser sintering technology.[11]Recently giant 3D Printers in China printed ten houses in one day and at a cost less that 5000 dollars per house, proving just how cost and time efficient 3D Printing can be.[12] Thus, these additive manufacturing machines can prove to be of extreme utility for creating something at your home or in a factory.

3D Printers for homes: Adrian Bowyer, who is known for his contribution to the 3D Printing industry, invented a home 3D Printer called the RepRap[13]. Interestingly, RepRap is a printer that can make its own parts and self-replicate thus, a RepRap printer can create another RepRap printer which is exactly similar to the original one. A person owning this printer can create and produce a variety of daily-use plastic objects like containers, glasses cutlery etc[14]. These printers many not produce high quality products but at a price that is drastically lower than the products brought from market. RepRap is a community project, and all its designs are available for everyone online. Anyone can make valuable additions or changes to the design using their own creative mind. The official website of RepRap has put on display the statistics of 2017, which shows that RepRap is the leading choice for private individuals and households among other high-end 3D Printer manufacturers like Stratasys, 3D Systems etc. This is mostly because of the huge cost difference between them and the maximum demand existing for a printer that could produce your daily use objects at almost zero cost.

[1]SuperMassiveTV, "A Brief History of 3D Printing - MakerBot vs Formlabs", *YouTube*. Online Video Clip, https://youtu.be/ T9d8mhGaOaw(Last Accessed on August 23, 2018).

[2]*History Of 3D Printing,* 3D PRINTING INDUSTRY: THE AUTHORITY ON 3D PRINTING, available at: https://3dprintingindustry.com/3d-printing-basics-free-beginners-guide#02-history. (Last Accessed on August 23, 2018).

[3]*About Makerbot 3D Printing,* MAKERBOT, available at: https://www.makerbot.com/about-us/ (Last accessed on 24th August, 2018).

[4]Kelly Clay, *3D Printing Company MakerBot Acquired In $604 Million Deal,* FORBES, June 19, 2013, 19:22, available at: https://www.forbes.com/sites/kellyclay/2013/06/19/3d-printing-company-makerbot-acquired-in-604-million-deal/#218ce4141ef8 (Last accessed on 24th August, 2018).

[5]NoblisNetwork, "3D Printing and the Future (or Demise) of Intellectual Property" by John Hornick", *YouTube,* Online Video Clip, available at: https://youtu.be/JoIjUKlwFkA(Last Accessed on August 24, 2018).

[6]TJ McCue, *Wohlers Report 2018: 3D Printer Industry Tops $7 Billion,* FORBES, June 4, 2018, 04:03, available at: https://www.forbes.com/sites/tjmccue/2018/06/04/wohlers-report-2018-3d-printer-industry-rises-21-percent-to-over-7-billion/#13225ed62d1a (Last accessed on 24th August, 2018).

[7]John Hornick and Dan Roland, *Many 3D Printing Patents Are Expiring Soon: Here's A Roundup And Overview Of Them,* 3D PRINTING INDUSTRY, December 29th2013, 12:04 a.m., available at: https://3dprintingindustry.com/news/many-3d-printing-patents-expiring-soon-heres-round-overview-21708/#comments. (Last accessed on 25th August, 2018).

[8]Vishal Makhija, *3D Printing – Opportunities, Challenges and the Future in India,* THE TECH PANDA, January 7, 2014, available at: https://thetechpanda.com/2014/01/07/3d-printing-opportunities-challenges-future-india/ (Last accessed on 25th August, 2018).

[9]Michael Weinberg, *IT WILL BE AWESOME IF THEY DON'T SCREW IT UP: 3D Printing, Intellectual Property, and the Fight Over the Next Great Disruptive Technology,* PUBLIC KNOWLEDGE, Novemeber 2010, available at: https://www.publicknowledge.org/files/docs/3DPrintingPaperPublicKnowledge.pdf(Last accessed on 25th August, 2018).

[10]"An open platform where all designs are encouraged to be licensed under a Creative Commons license, meaning that anyone can use or alter any design."*See:* THINGIVERSE - DIGITAL DESIGNS FOR PHYSICAL

OBJECTS, https://www.thingiverse.com/(Last accessed on 25th August, 2018).

[11]Simon Bradshaw; Adrian Bowyer; Patrick Haufe, *The Intellectual Property Implications of Low-Cost 3D Printing*, 7 SCRIPTed 5 (2010).

[12]Mashable, "What Is 3D Printing and How Does It Work? | Mashable Explains", *YouTube*, Online Video Club, available at: https://youtu.be/Vx0Z6LplaMU (Last accessed on 25th August, 2018).

[13]Dr. Adrian Bowyer, http://www.adrianbowyer.com/about.html (Last accessed on 25th August, 2018).

[14]Rep Rap, https://reprap.org/wiki/RepRap(Last accessed on 28th August, 2018).

CHAPTER FOUR

IMPLICATIONS ON INTELLECTUAL PROPERTY LAW

Gartner, a leading global research and advisory company, predicted and published in 2014 that, "by 2018, 3D printing will result in the loss of at least $100 billion per year in IP globally."[1] Yet, now that the year 2018 is coming to an end, there have not been any significant losses to IP resulting from 3D Printing industry. This could be because the growth of this industry, though promising, but has been slower than predicted and most of the world's population, residing in the third world countries, do not even know that such technology exists.[2] However, its implications on IP laws have been discussed by many academicians as well as industry specialists. One such personality is John Hornick, who has theorised reasons why IP laws will be adversely affected by the growth of 3D Printing industry[3]. He states that 3D Printing industry shall bring a paradigm shift in our traditional IP laws.

According to Hornick, 3D Printing would result in, what he calls, ***"democratization of manufacturing"***. Using 3D Printers, anyone could make anything at their homes and this would eliminate several stages involved in the traditional process of production of goods. There would be no barrier to entry in market, no need for distribution channels or retailers or shipping of products to the customers. In other words, with the evolution of 3D Printing industry, customers will also be manufacturers. Intellectual property, in such a scenario, would play an important role in protection of the data which is needed to print the 3D products. This data will constitute the design blueprints or the CAD files, and our present Copyright or Patent laws are not effective enough to protect this data. [4] 3D Printing, essentially would also lead to manufacturing *"away from control"*, which is another reason given by Hornick, for 3D printing to have detrimental effects on IP laws. Imagine a scenario where a person can create a beautiful piece of necklace designed by any of the leading fashion countries, by using a 3D printer at home, through downloadable blueprints of design available for free online at almost 1% of the cost of the original necklace. The fashion label will have no way of knowing about what a person is making at his home and thus will have no way of stopping him/her. This would result in copyright protection becoming more crucial to companies for protection of the blueprint designs of their products. However, when we look at the current state of affairs with respect to copyright protection for artistic works, the internet has been a massive hurdle, because of the sheer number of websites distributing pirated copies of books, movies or music available online for free[5]. Thus, the copyright laws will be drastically affected, as stricter provisions would be required for better protection of original design blueprints of the companies, to prevent infringement.

John Hornick has explained this attack on IP Laws by the 3D Printing industry, through what he calls the "five eyes (or I's)". *Infringement* of IP through increased amount of fake or pirated products being produced away from control; difficulty in *Identification* of any infringement that is happening away from control; enforcement of IP protection would become *Impractical* or *Impossible*, due to ineffective and inadequate IP laws; and, *Irrelevance* of IP rights, as they would not be able to guarantee protection of IP in practical effect. [6]

The above-mentioned view of the effect of 3D Printing industry on IP laws can be considered to be very grave and negative, as this would discourage any more start ups or small businesses to enter this industry. Another important concern is that this technology clashes with the traditional business models, as why would any industry want to sell a printer to a customer that would enable the customer to create almost any daily-use item, or the same printer itself at home, or any generic version of a branded product, as this could lead to potential disruption of mass production and several industries. Increase in democratization of manufacturing would ultimately result in manufacturing that is away from control, which would further lead to destruction of IP laws[7]. Since, 21st century is the age of digitization and the entire world is moving towards encouraging new innovations in technology for the advancement of mankind, 3D Printing technology cannot be ignored or dismissed, just because our laws have not matched the pace at which technology has developed.

Let us now move on to discussing the implications of this revolutionary technology on patents specifically, the current legal framework in USA and India, along with suggestions for improving the existing framework to incorporate the protection of IP rights in 3D Printing industry.

[1]Nick Hall, *IP Losses To Top $100 Billion In 2018*, 3D PRINTING INDUSTRY, 30th May, 2018, 11:03 a.m., available at: https://3dprintingindustry.com/news/ip-losses-top-100-billion-2018-80821/ (Last accessed on 28th August, 2018).

[2]*Gartner's Top 3 Failed Predictions on 3D Printing*, MEDIUM, 29th January, 2018, available at: https://medium.com/@3dpbm/gartners-top-3-failed-predictions-on-3d-printing-that-will-probably-never-come-true-ef8db62e70c3(Last accessed on 28th August, 2018).

[3]John Hornick, *3D Printing and IP Rights: The Elephant in the Room*, 55 Santa Clara L. Rev. 803 (2015).

[4]*Ibid.*

[5]*See:*Amrita Khalid and John-Michael Bond, *The 15 Best Torrent Sites Still Up And Running*, THE DAILY DOT, May 1, 2018 at 7:05PM, available at: https://www.dailydot.com/debug/best-torrent-sites/(Last accessed on 28th August, 2018).

[6]*Supra Note 20.*

[7]*Supra Note 8.*

CHAPTER FIVE

CHALLENGES TO LAW OF PATENTS

In 3D Printing arena, the CAD files, which are the blueprints of the objects that are to be 3D printed, are the main source of patent infringement. The CAD file is not merely a blueprint, but it is the device which would lead the customer to produce infringing products, just by the click of a button. The problem with these CAD files is that they are easily downloadable and sharable files, just like MP3 files and this could lead to mass indirect infringement of patents. As music and movies became easily available online through various file sharing websites like Bit Torrent, in MP3 or MP4 formats, their digitization has led to several copyright infringement cases. In the same manner, digitization of manufacturing could lead to large scale losses for the patent holders. Thus, 3D Printing would make it easier to copy products and as a result it would make infringement of patents easier.

1. POSITION UNDER USA'S PATENT LAW

The U.S. Patents Act essentially provides for two kinds of patent infringement: direct and indirect. Direct infringement is defined under Section 271(a) of the U.S. Patent Act and it states the following:

"whoever without authority makes, uses or sells any patented invention, within the United States during the term of the patent therefor, infringes the patent.[1]"

In the 3D printing scenario, direct infringement will arise when a person uses his home 3D printer to print a product that is identical to a patented product of a company, through a CAD file available via free file sharing websites. If the company whose patented product has been copied finds the infringer, it can claim damages for direct infringement as per the abovementioned provision under the Act, that is, "making a patented invention without authorization by the owner company". Claims made by the company in this scenario can either be for direct infringement via use of 3D Printer or direct infringement through the CAD file itself.[2]

Claiming direct infringement against the customer who used the 3D printer to print a patented product, is an approach that faces many challenges. The first and foremost challenge is that it would be extremely difficult for any patent owner to find the person who has printed out their patented invention via CAD files available online. This would mean tracking down each and every person who downloaded a CAD file, through an online file sharing platform, that consisted a blueprint of the identical infringing product and printed it at his/her home. Claiming damages and pursuing litigation against individuals would be a very cumbersome task and will not serve the purpose effectively. Ultimately, the companies could end up losing potential customers and damaging their public image.[3]Many scholars have compared this 3D printing effect with the digital music industry where individual infringement claims have been very minimal because of massive scale of pirated MP3 files being shared on online platforms for free. This massive scale of digitized infringement could not be prevented or reduced through existing copyright laws.[4]

The next option would be to claim direct infringement via CAD files, thereby suing the online platform for uploading CAD files which could be considered "identical" to the patented product. While finding the online forum where the CAD file was shared may not be a challenge, but the person or persons who shared the file on the platform could be. However, it is still a better approach to file infringement suit against the CAD file owners, as suing the end customer would lead to negative press for the companies owning the patented products.[5] Now the question that arises is whether a CAD file owner be sued for direct infringement under Section 271(a) of the Patents Act? The best justification for treating the CAD file as equivalent to the patented product is that one can easily obtain the copied or infringing product through a click of a button after they have downloaded the CAD file. The sale of the CAD file should amount to direct infringement as it is equivalent to having obtained the tangible product itself. However, this approach is also questionable since a CAD file can only amount to a tangible product if the customer actually prints it, and thus suing the owner of CAD file before the sale has actually been printed into a physical product, may not be the appropriate action.[6] Therefore, bringing action for direct infringement of the patented product against the end customer or the owner of CAD file, is not a fool proof approach and will not be of any help to the patent owners.

This brings us to the next category of infringement, that is, indirect infringement. As per the provisions of U.S. Patents Act, there are two types of indirect infringement – active inducement and contributory infringement.

Section 271(b) of the Patents Act states that,

"Whoever actively induces infringement of a patent shall be liable as an infringer."

Timothy R. Holbrook, a recognized patent scholar has stated in his paper on Patent Litigation and Strategy, *"Three things have to be proved to constitute active inducement of infringement:*

a. It must result into direct infringement of patent.
b. Specific intent to induce a third party to infringe.
c. Affirmative act on part of the infringer."[7]

Now, when it comes to proving active inducement in 3D printing arena, the owner of the patent will have to prove that the third party has directly infringed his patent by satisfying the conditions mentioned in Section 271(a)[8] for proving direct infringement. The problems with proving direct infringement will be similar to the ones stated above, that is, finding the actual infringer of patent. Digital piracy makes the process of finding the actual infringer a very lengthy and difficult process. If the patent holder is able to prove through circumstantial evidence, that the CAD file has been downloaded and printed and the infringing item has been "made", direct infringement could be constituted. However, it is again a challenge to analyse whether circumstantial evidence is enough to prove infringement specially in the area of software related invention. Assuming that the existence of direct infringement has been proved, the patent holder would have to prove the existence of intent, that is, the CAD file owner must have the knowledge that he is distributing the blueprint of a patented product. This would again pose a major challenge for the patent holders because of the peer to peer file sharing platforms where large number of unsophisticated users upload files for others to download. These users and uploaders of CAD files may not be aware of the existence of patents, and even though ignorance of law cannot be a defence, proving the intention of inducing infringement would be a herculean task.[9]

The next type of indirect infringement has been defined under Section 271(c) of the U.S. Patents Act, which states that:

*"Whoever sells a component of a patented machine, manufacture, combination or composition, or a material or apparatus for use in practicing a patented process, constituting a material part of the invention, knowing the same to be especially made or especially adapted for use in an infringement of such patent, and not a staple article or commodity of commerce suitable for substantial non-infringing use, shall be liable as a contributory infringer."***[10]**

It would be much easier for the patent holder to sue the CAD file owner for contributory infringement rather than direct infringement or active inducement. This is because, in contributory infringement, the intention of the infringer can be proved simply by establishing that a) he is aware of the patent and b) he does not have any "substantial non-infringing use".[11] By reading the section 271(c) clearly, one can observe that there is no specific requirement of proving the intention of the infringer. The intention can be presumed if the accused infringer is aware of the patent and has no other substantial non-infringing use for the patent.[12] To establish a claim of contributory infringement under Section 271(c), the following requirements have to be fulfilled: a) the accused must be offering to sell, selling or importing into U.S., b) a component of the patented product, c) knowing the component to be especially adapted for use in an infringement of apatent with no substantial non-infringing uses, and d) which results in an act of direct infringement.[13]

In a scenario where the patent holder wants to sue the owner/distributor of the CAD file for contributary infringement; by judging the first requirement under Section 271(c), that is, if the CAD file owner/distributor "sells" or "offers to sell", the first requirement would be satisfied, as making a CAD file available of an online platform would amount to offer or sale. However, the problem with this approach is that the CAD files cost very less or almost nothing when made available on a peer to peer (P2P) file sharing online forum. Thus, if the CAD file is available for free, there is no consideration and thus whether it will amount to sale or offer of sale within the meaning under 271(c), is the dilemma.[14]

Adding to the difficulty, the second question on the requirement of "component"is, whether a CAD file can be considered as a component of the patented product. A component means a physical part of the patented device which is crucial to its functioning. So, if that part is being sold by the accused, then he would be liable for contributory infringement. CAD files are digital files that are actually the representation of the entire patented product itself. The interpretation of word "component", under section 271(f)[15], which runs parallel to Sections 271(b) and (c), was discussed in the case *Microsoft Corp. v. AT&T Corp.[16]*, wherein the questionable "component" was a software of AT&T Corp. for digitally encoding and compressing recorded speech, which was transported by Microsoft to a foreign country. The software alone was not an infringing object, but when it was uploaded in a computer it amounted to direct infringement. The Court held that, software "in the abstract" will not be a component, but a software loaded in a "medium (including CDs or other forms of memory storage)" could amount to a component. A software that only provides instructions will not form a component of the end product, but a software which when stored on a medium can amount to component. And, thus a CAD file can be considered to be a component when encoded on a medium.[17] However, a CAD file when printed using the 3D printer becomes the entire product, so Microsoft case still does not give a clear picture whether CAD files can be considered as components or not.[18]

Repair and Construction Doctrine: This doctrine basically emerges from the right of the customers to use a patented product freely, once they have bought the product from the patent owner. And so, when the patented product malfunctions or breaks down, the customers also have the right to repair it and use replacement parts to make it functioning again. The problem with 3D printing industry is that, it makes manufacturing small parts of a machinery very easy. While customers can create their own new products easily using a 3D printer, they can certainly create broken parts of patented products at home and fix them. For example, a popular YouTube personality, Joel Telling, going by the account name "3D Printing Nerd"[19], shows just how easily persons sitting at home can create daily use objects and even repair parts for their broken products. In one interesting video, Joel 3D prints a small bracket for his refrigerator that has broken, which helps the doors of his refrigerator open and shut easily.[20] The acceptable position under law is that, a customer can make a non-patented part of a patented product for repair purposes or for replacing the broken part, but the problem arises when a customer makes several parts of a patented product simultaneously that results in modifications to existing product. Current patent law states that a customer is allowed to repair a patented product, but not reconstruct it. As 3D printing technology advances, customers will be less dependent of traditional manufacturing techniques for repair parts or "any" parts for that matter, and numerous cases for piracy and infringing usage may arise before the court. Thus, a proper differentiation between standards of repair and reconstruction are required to be established, to clarify the position of the doctrine under patent law.[21]

- **DIGITAL INFRINGEMENT IN A P2P AGE: A Peep into Copyright Protection Against Infringement in Light Of - MGM v. Grokster[22]**

Since, 3D printing industry would be potentially based on using the Peer to Peer file sharing platform for distribution of CAD files, it is important to study this interesting case that clarifies the current position of law with respect to contributory infringement by owners of P2P file sharing platforms. *Thingiverse[23]* and *Shapeways[24]* are the two currently popular open sharing websites where the users can create and share design blueprints in the form of CAD file for 3D printable objects. However, what happens when users start creating blueprints of potentially infringing patented products and start sharing them on these platforms? Peer-to-peer mechanism provides an easier and efficient online system for sharing of files wherein copies of a particular file is stored in several computers and can be supplied by any of those computers on a peer request for that file. This prevents loss of data thus making it an efficient data sharing and storing mechanism. Though, as the copies of files are stored on a huge number of different computers, finding the best and original source of the file becomes difficult. BitTorrent, Piratebay etc. are few websites for file sharing platforms which provide massive number of pirated digital files of books, movies and music.[25]

Principles of secondary liability do not allow products that enable copyright infringement. In the case *Sony Corp. of America v. Universal City Studios, Inc.,*[26] the court imported the specific provision for indirect infringement under section 271[27] of the Patents Act in Copyright Law to create a "parallel substantial non-infringing rule" under copyright law. Sony's VCRs (video cassette recorders) were being used by several customers to record the telecast of television programmes, whose copyright owners were the Universal City Studios, for later viewing. Universal claimed contributory infringement of copyright by Sony, however the court held Sony, not liable as their product was being used for non-infringing usage.[28]

After Sony[29], came the Napster[30] case in 2001. Napster was a peer-to-peer file sharing website, where compressed digital music files were shared with ease due to its "centralised server system that indexed connected users and filesavailable on their machines, creating a searchable list of music available acrossNapster's network." The defence of *Fair Use* by Napster was rejected on the grounds that "repeated and exploitative use of copyrighted material would amount to infringement even if it was not offered for sale". With regards to Contributory Infringement, the courts decided that Napster certainly had knowledge of actual infringement on the website, and moreover the lack of efforts taken by it to reduce infringement plus the financial benefits that Napster was earning, made it liable for contributing to infringement.[31]

In *MGM Studios Inc. v. Grokster[32]*, the defendants were the creators of a P2P file sharing website, similar to Napster[33], which was largely used for sharing copyrighted musical works, many of which belonged to the plaintiffs, MGM. They were distributing the software for free and several known figures of the recording label industry sued them for vicarious copyright liability. The court decided that the doctrine behind Sony[34]'s decision was not enough for this case, as the huge amount of infringing activity could not be overlooked on the grounds of "substantial non-infringing uses". The court essentially imported the active inducement analogy from patent law and decided upon a cause of action, stating that if there is evidence against the accused of unlawful intent to promote infringement of copyrightable works, along with knowledge, then he shall be liable for actively inducing infringement of copyrights. The court found sufficient reasons to hold Grokster liable for unlawful intent behind allowing sharing of copyrighted works of their website, and thus held them liable for inducing infringement. By not following the doctrine established in Sony case, and creating a new standard for inducement of infringement under copyright law, the court has provided copyright owners with a powerful stance against P2P websites.[35]The question is, whether the Grokster decision has reduced infringement, or has simply slowed the P2P technology temporarily. Websites like BitTorrent and The Pirate Bay continue to fight the copyright owners over the future of file sharing.

- *CAD Files, meet iTunes! – Combined Protection of Patent and Copyrights:*

Many academicians have found the solution of the problem of patent infringement because of 3D printing by proposing a combination of protection through patent as well as copyrights.[36] If we look at the music and movie industries, there has been a huge growth in media service providers such as Netflix[37], Hulu[38] or iTunes[39], that provide access to authentic and licensed copyrighted musical and dramatic works at a reasonable price. People do prefer to buy authentic products that are original versions and available at reasonable price, rather than going for pirated copies.[40] Imagine creating a similar mechanism for CAD files. The established copyright law with respect to digital file sharing devices, as well as the added protection under DMCA which was specifically instituted to reduce digital infringement can provide better protection to CAD files which may not be possible under Patent law. Also, copyright protection will incentivise the sharing the CAD files online through a mechanism similar to iTunes, as stated above, where in copyright owners of CAD files could sell them to customers at an affordable price. Meanwhile, the product that the CAD fie will enable to be 3D printed, shall already be protected under the patent law.

This combined protection mechanism may seem like an appropriate solution; however, the current patent or copyright laws are not eligible to incorporate this solution. CAD, files are purely functional works that are excluded from copyright protection.[41] The test of novelty under copyright law is also different, as copyright laws only protect original works and do not focus on the novelty aspect of works. So, someone can eventually take an idea from the copyrighted CAD file and makes certain changes to it, claiming a copyright over the modified version of CAD file, on the basis of skill, labour and originality applied by the person. But when that CAD file is 3D printed, it will evidently infringe the patented product as it will not be novel.

3D Printable products would therefore need a two-fold protection, that is, the end product being protected by patent and the CAD file which is the digital blueprint being protected by copyright, with the product satisfying the conditions for protection under both patent as well as copyright. Thus, existing patent and copyright laws need to be modified in order to incorporate an efficient mechanism to prevent infringement by 3D printing technology.

2. PROTECTION UNDER INDIAN PATENT LAW (OR COPYRIGHT LAW?)

The Indian Patents Act, 1970 does not have any exclusive provision for contributory infringement or indirect infringement, and this would make it very difficult for dealing with potential large-scale infringement as the 3D printing industry expands worldwide. However, the CAD files can be protected under Copyright Law, as a literary work because it is in the form of software. Actually, a CAD file will only be given protection under Copyright laws in India as patent protection for software is excluded under section 3(k) of Indian Patents Act. Therefore, only the end product could be protected by Patent Law in India. This could actually work for the 3D Printing industry, if a combined protection model through patent and copyright law is already available in India. Though the question that arises is, how well can the existing copyright laws of India protect the infringement of CAD files, so as to prevent further infringement of the patented products.

USA ratified the WIPO internet treaties[42] in 1998 and enacted the Digital Millennium Copyright Act (DMCA)[43].It was passed to protect the extensive and wide spread infringement of copyrights over the internet. Section 512[44] of the Act which provides for liability for online copyright infringement, was inserted with a view to encourage the economic growth of online entertainment industry and also protect the rights of innovators and creators. According to this provision, if any owner of copyrighted material finds any content on a website infringing her copyright, she has the right to submit a notice to the Internet Service Provider (ISP) to take down the infringing material immediately. This "notice and takedown" procedure was introduced for dealing with the online infringement of copyrighted movies, music, books etc., effectively. However, the "knowledge" requirement is still crucial, that is, this procedure can only be initiated if the ISP did not have actual knowledge of the infringing activity or material on its website and does not receive a financial benefit for the infringing material. It provides a chance or a "safe harbour" for the ISP to take down the infringing content on notice and avoid further action or litigation. The current judicial position on this requirement is clear and says that if there is actual knowledge, then there shall be active inducement/contributory infringement on part of the service provider.[45]

Similar kind of provisions are enacted in the IT Act, 2000 of India under Section 79[46] which was given a wider scope through the 2011 guidelines[47]. An "intermediary" as defined under section 2(w)[48] of the Act, includes anyone who stores or transmits a message that is infringing on behalf of a third person. The 2011 guidelines provide that the intermediaries impose certain rules and regulations on customers that stop them from uploading or downloading any infringing material on their website. And if any person finds infringing material online they can complain to the intermediary and ask to take it down. However, the complaint mechanism is not very strict and enforceable as the Act does not provide for the intermediary to respond to the complaint. Thus, need for stricter provisions has to be acknowledged.[49]The position in Indian Copyright Law, on contributory infringement found in section 51(a)(ii) of the Copyright Act, 1957, is not clear or broad enough to incorporate sufficient protection against digital piracy. However, Delhi High Court in the case *My Space Inc. vs Super Cassettes Industries Ltd.*[50], applied this section and

CAD files can only be protected effectively under copyright laws if it is capable to prevent large scale digital infringement, or else it could lead to large scale patent infringement cases. In both USA and India, the prevention of infringement through 3D printing can only happen if the copyright laws are adequate in protecting from digital infringement so that the copying of patented products by printing the CAD file using the 3D printer can be prevented.

[1]U.S. Patent Law, 35 U.S.C. § 271(a) (2012).

[2]Tabrez Y. Ebrahim, *3D Printing: Digital Infringement & Digital Regulation*, 14 Nw. J. Tech. & Intell. Prop. 46 (2016).

[3]Timothy R. Holbrook; Lucas S. Osborn, *Digital Patent Infringement in an Era of 3D Printing*, 48 U.C.D. L. Rev. 1364 (2015)

[4]*Ibid.*

[5]*Id.*

[6]*Supra Note 26.*

[7]*Supra Note 27.*

[8]U.S. Patent Law, 35 U.S.C. § 271(a) (2012).

[9]*Supra Note 30.*

[10]U.S. Patent Law, 35 U.S.C. § 271(c) (2012).

[11]*Ibid.*

[12]*Id.*

[13]*Supra Note 31;*U.S. Patent Law, 35 U.S.C. § 271(c) (2012).

[14]*Id.*

[15] See U.S. Patent Law, 35 U.S.C. § 271(f) (2012).

[16]Microsoft Corp. v. AT&T Corp., 550 U.S. 437 (2007).

[17]*Supra Note 37.*

[18]*Id.*

[19]3D Printing Nerd, "3D Printing Nerd – Channel Trailer", *YouTube*, Online Video Clip, https://youtu.be/TMlF8bl4MdQ (Last accessed on 1st September, 2018).

[20]3D Printing Ner d, "My Top 5 Useful 3D Prints", *YouTube*, Online Video Clip, https://youtu.be/3BDK5Wz53Ig (Last accessed on 1st September, 2018).

[21]Kelsey B. Wilbanks, *The Challenges of 3D Printing to the Repair-Reconstruction Doctrine in Patent Law*, 20 Geo. Mason L. Rev. 1175 (2013).

[22]MGM Studios Inc. v. Grokster, Ltd., 125 S. Ct. 2764, 2771 (2005).

[23] See THINGIVERSE, https://www.thingiverse.com/.

[24] See SHAPEWAYS, https://www.shapeways.com/.

[25]*Understanding P2P File Sharing*, LIFEWIRE, available at: https://www.lifewire.com/definition-of-p2p-818026(Last accessed on 1st September, 2018).

[26]Sony Corp. of America v. Universal City Studios, Inc. 464 U.S. 417 (1984).

[27] See U.S. Patent Law, 35 U.S.C. § 271(2012).

[28]Galen Hancock, Metro-Goldwyn-Mayer Studios Inc. v. Grokster, Ltd.: Inducing Infringement and Secondary Copyright Liability, 21 Berkeley Tech. L.J. 189 (2006).

[29]Supra Note 50.

[30] A&M Records, Inc. v. Napster, Inc., 239 F.3d 1004 (2001).

[31]*Case Study: A&M Records, Inc. v. Napster, Inc.*, WASHINGTON UNIVERSITY OF LAW, August 01, 2013, available at: https://onlinelaw.wustl.edu/blog/case-study-am-records-inc-v-napster-inc/ (Last Accessed on 2nd September, 2018).

[32]MGM Studios Inc. v. Grokster, Ltd., 125 S. Ct. 2764, 2771 (2005).

[33]A&M Records, Inc. v. Napster, Inc., 239 F.3d 1004 (2001).

[34]Sony Corp. of America v. Universal City Studios, Inc. 464 U.S. 417 (1984).

[35]Supra Note 52.

[36]See: Timothy R. Holbrook; Lucas S. Osborn, Digital Patent Infringement in an Era of 3D Printing, 48 U.C.D. L. Rev. 1319 (2015); Frank Ward, Parents & 3D Printing: Protecting the Democratization of Manufacturing by Combining Existing Intellectual Property Protections, 25 DePaul J. Art Tech. & Intell. Prop. L 91 (2014).

[37]NETFLIX, ("Netflix, Inc. is an American over-the-top media services provider, headquartered in Los Gatos, California." See: https://www.netflix.com.).

[38]HULU ("Hulu is an American entertainment company that provides over-the-top media services owned by Hulu LLC, a joint venture with The Walt Disney Company, 21st Century Fox, Comcast, and AT&T.", see: Hulu.com).

[39]iTunes, ("iTunes is a media player, media library, Internet radio broadcaster, and mobile device management application developed by Apple Inc.", see: apple.com/itunes).

[40]Frank Ward, Parents & 3D Printing: Protecting theDemocratization of Manufacturing by Combining ExistingIntellectual Property Protections, 25 DePaul J. ArtTech. & Intell. Prop. L 91 (2014).

[41]*Ibid.*

[42]*WIPO Internet Treaties*, WIPO, available at: http://www.wipo.int/copyright/en/activities/internet_treaties.html (Last Accessed on 2nd September, 2018).

[43]Digital Millennium Copyright Act (DMCA), 1998.

[44]U.S. Copyright Law, 17 U.S.C. § 512.

[45]Aakanksha Kumar, *Internet Intermediary (ISP) Liability for Contributory Copyright Infringement in USA and India: Lack of Uniformity as A Trade Barrier*, Journal of Intellectual Property Rights, Vol 19, pp 274 (2014).

[46]Information Technology Act, 2000, Section 79.

[47]The Information Technology (Intermediaries guidelines) Rules, 2011, available at: http://www.wipo.int/edocs/lexdocs/laws/en/in/in099en.pdf.

[48]*Ibid.*

[49]*Id.*

[50]Myspace Inc. vs. Super Cassettes Industries Ltd., 2017(69) PTC 1.

CHAPTER SIX

CONCLUSIONS AND SUGGESTIONS

Looking at the underlying technology and working of a 3D printer, it is clear that IP law is going to affect almost every step of the process. The effects on patent litigation will be very challenging as the present laws are not equipped to incorporate protection for infringements of CAD files, surprisingly, both in USA and India. Online content distributors also adopt Digital Rights Management (DRM) techniques to prevent unauthorized usage of copyrighted content available on their websites by the end customers. They use several technical solutions like digital locks or encryption of data to preventing piracy and ensuring that the rights of copyright holders are protected. Some examples of content providers that use DRM are Amazon Ebooks, Netflix, etc.[1] However, most of the big players in this market have given up on DRM, putting too many precautionary measures ultimately drives away the end users. Apple had an on-going debate with the RIAA (Record Industry Association of America), that if they allow licensed music to be sold on iTunes, Apple would remove get rid of the DRM.[2] The problems with DRM are mainly that it doesn't work that well and "cripples the functionality" of the devices providing content.[3] Thus, DRM might be a waste of time and money for securing protection of CAD files if it has not worked well in other areas.

As the settled law in USA, contributory infringement claim against P2P websites would only work if the service providers had "knowledge" of the infringing activity/content available on their websites. Removing any file from the website whenever a patent owner raises a complaint that the end product is too similar to his patented product is impractical as it would basically drive the users away from the website. Enforcement of laws against patent infringement will be futile against a customer manufacturing something at home using a 3D printer, and so ultimately an exemption from infringement may have to be devised for uses of a personal 3D printer.

A DMCA- like authority for patents could also create a balance between the right holders and intermediary websites. Such changes need to be brought in the existing laws for developing a balanced enforcement framework that allows technology like 3D printing to grow without harming the interests of right holder.

[1]Divij Joshi, *Should DRM be an Integral Part of the Open Web?*, SPICY IP, April 19, 2017, available at: https://spicyip.com/2017/04/spicyip-fellowship-2017-18-should-drm-be-an-integral-part-of-the-open-web.html (Last Accessed on 3rd September 2018).

[2]*How FairPlay Works: Apple's iTunes DRM Dilemma*, ROUGHLYDRAFTED, February 26, 2007, available at: http://www.roughlydrafted.com/RD/RDM.Tech.Q1.07/2A351C60-A4E5-4764-A083-FF8610E66A46.html(Last Accessed on 3rd September 2018).

[3]Michael Weinberg, *DRM on 3D Printers is a Big Deal. Nathan Myhrvold's Patent is Not*, PUBLIC KNOWLEDGE, October 22, 2012, available at: https://www.publicknowledge.org/news-blog/blogs/drm-3d-printers-big-deal-nathan-myhrvolds-pat (Last Accessed on 3rd September 2018).

www.ingramcontent.com/pod-product-compliance
Lightning Source LLC
Chambersburg PA
CBHW072144150726
48002CB00004B/1618